THE CARPENTERED HEN

THE CARPENTERED HEN

and other tame creatures

POEMS BY

JOHN UPDIKE

HARPER & ROW, PUBLISHERS

New York and Evanston

11/1970
Am-Lit.

Of the fifty-five poems in this book, thirty-eight, and E, J, M, and Q of "A Cheerful Alphabet of Pleasant Objects," appeared originally in *The New Yorker.*

"The One-Year-Old" first appeared in the March, 1957, issue of *The Ladies' Home Journal.* Copyright 1957 by The Curtis Publishing Company.

"Recitative for Punished Products" first appeared in the February 9, 1955, issue of *Punch.* Reprinted by permission of *Punch.*

"A Modest Mound of Bones" and "Ode III.ii : Horace" were first published in *Commonweal* on April 26 and June 7, 1957, respectively. Reprinted by permission of The Commonweal Publishing Co., Inc.

"A Wooden Darning Egg" first appeared in the December, 1956, issue of *Harper's Magazine* and is reprinted with their permission.

Library of Congress catalog card number: 58-6158

To Mary

CONTENTS

When she [Philosophy] saw that the Muses of poetry were present by my couch giving words to my lamenting, she was stirred a while; her eyes flashed fiercely, and said she, "Who has suffered these seducing mummers to approach this sick man? Never do they support those in sorrow by any healing remedies, but rather do ever foster the sorrow by poisonous sweets. These are they who stifle the fruit-bearing harvest of reason with the barren briars of the passions: they free not the minds of men from disease, but accustom them thereto."

—BOETHIUS, DE CONSOLATIONE PHILOSOPHIAE

THE CARPENTERED HEN

DUET, WITH MUFFLED BRAKE DRUMS

50 Years Ago Rolls met Royce—a Meeting that made
Engineering History
                              —*advertisement in* The New Yorker

Where gray walks slope through shadows shaped like lace
Down to dimpleproof ponds, a precious place
Where birds of porcelain sing as with one voice
Two gold and velvet notes—there Rolls met Royce.

"Hallo," said Rolls. His umber silhouette
Seemed mounted on a blotter brushed when wet
To indicate a park. Beyond, a brown
Line hinted at the profile of The Town.

And Royce, his teeth and creases straight, his eye
A perfect match for that well-lacquered sky
(Has zenith since, or iris, been so pure?),
Responded, "Pleased to meet you, I am sure."

A graceful pause, then Rolls, the taller, spake:
"Ah—is there anything you'd care to make?
A day of it? A fourth at bridge? Some tea?"
Royce murmured, "If your afternoon is free,
I'd rather, much, make engineering history."

1

EX-BASKETBALL PLAYER

Pearl Avenue runs past the high-school lot,
Bends with the trolley tracks, and stops, cut off
Before it has a chance to go two blocks,
At Colonel McComsky Plaza. Berth's Garage
Is on the corner facing west, and there,
Most days, you'll find Flick Webb, who helps Berth out.

Flick stands tall among the idiot pumps—
Five on a side, the old bubble-head style,
Their rubber elbows hanging loose and low.
One's nostrils are two S's, and his eyes
An E and O. And one is squat, without
A head at all—more of a football type.

Once Flick played for the high-school team, the Wizards.
He was good: in fact, the best. In '46
He bucketed three hundred ninety points,
A county record still. The ball loved Flick.
I saw him rack up thirty-eight or forty
In one home game. His hands were like wild birds.

He never learned a trade, he just sells gas,
Checks oil, and changes flats. Once in a while,
As a gag, he dribbles an inner tube,
But most of us remember anyway.
His hands are fine and nervous on the lug wrench.
It makes no difference to the lug wrench, though.

Off work, he hangs around Mae's luncheonette.
Grease-gray and kind of coiled, he plays pinball,
Smokes those thin cigars, nurses lemon phosphates.
Flick seldom says a word to Mae, just nods
Beyond her face toward bright applauding tiers
Of Necco Wafers, Nibs, and Juju Beads.

PLAYER PIANO

My stick fingers click with a snicker
And, chuckling, they knuckle the keys;
Light-footed, my steel feelers flicker
And pluck from these keys melodies.

My paper can caper; abandon
Is broadcast by dint of my din,
And no man or band has a hand in
The tones I turn on from within.

At times I'm a jumble of rumbles,
At others I'm light like the moon,
But never my numb plunker fumbles,
Misstrums me, or tries a new tune.

SHIPBORED

That line is the horizon line.
The blue above it is divine.
The blue below it is marine.
Sometimes the blue below is green.

Sometimes the blue above is gray,
Betokening a cloudy day.
Sometimes the blue below is white,
Foreshadowing a windy night.

Sometimes a drifting coconut
Or albatross adds color, but
The blue above is mostly blue.
The blue below and I are, too.

AN ODE

FIRED INTO BEING BY LIFE'S 48-STAR EDITORIAL,
"WANTED: AN AMERICAN NOVEL"

STROPHE

Ours is the most powerful nation in the world. It has had a decade of unparalleled prosperity. Yet it is still producing a literature which sounds sometimes as if it were written by an unemployed homosexual. . . .

ANTISTROPHE

> I'm going to write a novel, hey,
>   I'll write it as per *Life*:
> I'm going to say "What a splendid day"
>   And "How I love my wife!"
> Let heroines be once again
>   Pink, languid, soft, and tall,
> For from my pen shall flow forth men
>   Heterosexual.

EPODE

Atomic fear or not, the incredible accomplishments of our day are surely the raw stuff of saga.

STROPHE

> Raw stuff shall be the stuff of which
>   My saga will be made:
> Brown soil, black pitch, the lovely rich,

6

The noble poor, the raid
On Harpers Ferry, Bunker Hill,
    Forefathers fairly met,
The home, the mill, the hearth, the Bill
    Of Rights, et cet., et cet.

Nobody wants a Pollyanna literature.

I shan't play Pollyanna, no,
    I'll stare facts in the eye:
Folks come and go, experience woe,
    And, when they're tired, die.
Unflinchingly, I plan to write
    A book to comprehend
Rape, fury, spite, and, burning bright,
    A sunset at The End.

In every healthy man there is a wisdom deeper than his conscious mind, reaching beyond memory to the primeval rivers, a yea-saying to the goodness and joy of life.

A wise and not unhealthy man,
    I'm telling everyone
That deeper than the old brainpan
    Primeval rivers run;
For *Life* is joy and *Time* is gay
    And *Fortune* smiles on those
Good books that say, at some length, "Yea,"
    And thereby spite the Noes.

7

THE CLAN

Emlyn reads in Dickens' clothes.
Tennessee writes fleshy prose;
William Carlos, bony poems.
Esther swims in hippodromes.
Ted likes hits but hates his fans;
Gluyas draws Americans.
Vaughan pens music, score on score;
Soapy is a governor.
I trust everybody is
Thankful for the Williamses.

WHY THE TELEPHONE WIRES DIP AND THE POLES
ARE CRACKED AND CROOKED

The old men say
young men in gray
hung this thread across our plains
acres and acres ago.

But we, the enlightened, know
in point of fact it's what remains
of the flight of a marvellous crow
no one saw:
Each pole, a caw.

THE POPULATION OF ARGENTINA

[with T.D.E., 1952]

The Rand McNally Co.:
How little does it know!
  How much those clerks have missed
  Who blithely list
Argentina's pop. as four-
Teen million, and no more,
  And even slightly less!
Why, I can count
Twice that amount
  By skimming through the columns of the daily press.

For every new edition
  Sees another harried soul
Seek a haven from sedition,
  Flee assassins, jump parole,
Or escape a harsh decision
  Of the anti-vice patrol
    By visiting that vast arena
    Of refugees called Argentina.

On the pampas, it is certain,
Lounges Richard Haliburton,
Adolf Hitler, Martha Ray,
Leon Trotsky's ex-valet,
Greta Garbo, Mildred Fletcher,

"Fingers" Pico—you can bet your
Bottom dollar they are there,
Inhaling *bueno* air,
     As well
As all the aunts of Sun Yat-sen,
     The ten
Lost Tribes of Israel,
     Side by side
With every Balkan prince who never died.

Rand, recount; recount, McNally:
There's been some slip-up in your tally;
   Count Argentinian heads again.
Search every cellar, scan each alley,
And you'll discover Axis Sally
   Playing poker with Hart Crane.

EVEN EGRETS ERR

Egregious was the egret's error, very.
   Egressing from a swamp, the bird eschewed
No egriot (a sour kind of cherry) *
   It saw, and reaped extremest egritude.§

* Obs.
§ Rare form of obs. Aegritude, meaning sickness.

SCENIC

O when in San Francisco do
As natives do: they sit and stare
And smile and stare again. The view
Is visible from anywhere.

Here hills are white with houses whence,
Across a multitude of sills,
The owners, lucky residents,
See other houses, other hills.

The meanest San Franciscan knows,
No matter what his past has been,
There are a thousand patios
Whose view he is included in.

The Golden Gate, the cable cars,
Twin Peaks, the Spreckels habitat,
The local ocean, sun, and stars—
When fog falls, one admires *that*.

Here homes are stacked in such a way
That every picture window has
An unmarred prospect of the Bay
And, in its center, Alcatraz.

TUNE, IN AMERICAN TYPE

Set and printed in Great Britain by Tonbridge Print-
ers, Ltd., Peach Hall Works, Tonbridge, in Times nine
on ten point, on paper made by John Dickenson at
Croxley, and bound by James Burn at Esher.
   —*colophon in a book published by Michael Joseph (London)*

Ah, to be set and printed in
Great Britain now that Tonbridge Prin-
ters, Limited, employ old John
Dickenson, at Croxley. On
his pages is Times nine-on-ten-
point type impressed, and, lastly, when
at Peach Hall Works the job is done,
James Burn at Esher's job's begun.

> *Hey nonny nonny nonny,*
> *Hey nonny nonny nay!*

Tonbridge! Croxley! Esher! Ah,
is there, in America,
a tome contrived in such sweet towns?
No. English, English are the downs
where Jim Burn, honest craftsman, winds
beneath his load of reams; he binds
the sheets that once John Dickenson
squeezed flat from British pulp. *Hey non-*

> *ny nonny,* etc.

14

LAMENT, FOR COCOA

The scum has come.
  My cocoa's cold.
The cup is numb,
  And I grow old.

It seems an age
  Since from the pot
It bubbled, beige
  And burning hot—

Too hot to be
  Too quickly quaffed.
Accordingly,
  I found a draft

And in it placed
  The boiling brew
And took a taste
  Of toast or two.

Alas, time flies
  And minutes chill;
My cocoa lies
  Dull brown and still.

How wearisome!
  In likelihood,
The scum, once come,
  Is come for good.

RECITATIVE FOR PUNISHED PRODUCTS

I was once a tire. To bolster sales
My cunning maker filled me full of nails.
My treads were shredded. I was made a flat
By great machines designed to do just that.

I was a typewriter. Harsh was my test.
Ten years I toiled unoiled without a rest.
One billion times, so claim the pedagogues,
The quick brown foxes jumped my lazy cogs.

I used to be a watch. My tick and tock
Were interchanged by polychronic shock.
The bit of bounce my spring retained was sapped
By tales of clocks alarmed, of watches strapped.

I am a shears. My thin lips prophesy
The Day to Come when angles cloud the sky,
When rugs rise up, mute tools get out of hand,
And crazed computers walk the frenzied land.

All:
Awesome the clangs will be, fearful the whirs
When products punish manufacturers.

V. B. NIMBLE, V. B. QUICK

Science, Pure and Applied, by V. B. Wigglesworth,
F.R.S., Quick Professor of Biology in the University of
Cambridge.

—a talk listed in the B.B.C. Radio Times

V. B. Wigglesworth wakes at noon,
Washes, shaves, and very soon
Is at the lab; he reads his mail,
Tweaks a tadpole by the tail,
Undoes his coat, removes his hat,
Dips a spider in a vat
Of alkaline, phones the press,
Tells them he is F. R. S.,
Subdivides six protocells,
Kills a rat by ringing bells,
Writes a treatise, edits two
Symposia on "Will Man Do?,"
Gives a lecture, audits three,
Has the Sperm Club in for tea,
Pensions off an aging spore,
Cracks a test tube, takes some pure
Science and applies it, finds
His hat, adjusts it, pulls the blinds,
Instructs the jellyfish to spawn,
And, by one o'clock, is gone.

17

SONG OF THE OPEN FIREPLACE

When silly Sol in winter roisters
And roasts us in our closed-up cloisters
Like hosts of out-of-season oysters,
    The logs glow red.

When Sol grows cool and solely caters
To polar bears and figure skaters
And homes are turned refrigerators,
    The flames are dead.

And when idyllically transpires
The merger every man desires
Of air that nips and wood that fires,
    It's time for bed.

MARCH: A BIRTHDAY POEM
for Elizabeth

My child as yet unborn, the doctors nod,
Agreeing that your first month shall be March,
A time of year I know by heart and like
To talk about—I too was born in March.

March, like November a month largely unloved,
Parades before April, who steals all shows
With his harlequinade of things renewed.
Impatient for that pastel fool's approach,
Our fathers taunted March, called him *Hlyd-monath*,
Though the month is mild, and a murmurer.
Indeed, after the Titan's fall and shatter
Of February, March seems a silence.
The Romans, finding February's ruins
At the feet of March, heard his wind as boasting
And hailed his guilt with a war-god's name.

As above some street in a cobbled sea-town
From opposing walls two huge boards thrust
To advertise two inns, so do the signs
Of Pisces the Fish and Aries the Ram
Overhang March. Depending on the day,
Your fortunate gem shall be the bloodstone
Or the diamond, your lucky color crimson
Or silver gray. You shall prove affable,

Impulsive, lucky in your friends, or cross,
According to the counterpoint of stars.
So press your business ventures, wear cravats,
And swear not by the moon. If you plant wheat,
Do it at dawn. The same for barley. Let
The tide transplant kohlrabi, leeks, and beans.
Toward the month's end, sow hardy annuals.

It was this month when Caesar fell, Stalin died,
And Beethoven. In this month snowflakes melt—
Those last dry crusts that huddle by the barn.
Now kites and crocuses are hoisted up.
Doors slap open. Dogs snuffle soggy leaves,
Rehearsing rusty repertoires of smells.
The color of March is the one that lies
On the shadow side of young tree trunks.

March is no land of extremes. Dull as life,
It offers small flowers and minor holidays.
Clouds stride sentry and hold our vision down.
By much the same token, agonized roots
Are hidden by earth. Much, much is opaque.
The thunder bluffs, wind cannot be gripped,
And kites and crocuses are what they are.
Still, child, it is far from a bad month,
For all its weight of compromise and hope.
As modest as a monk, March shall be there
When on that day without a yesterday
You, red and blind and blank, gulp the air.

SUNFLOWER

Sunflower, of flowers
the most lonely,
yardstick of hours,
long-term stander
in empty spaces,
shunner of bowers,
indolent bender
seldom, in only
the sharpest of showers:
tell us, why
is it your face is
a snarl of jet swirls
and gold arrows, a burning
old lion face high
in a cornflower sky,
yet by turning
your head, we find
you wear a girl's
bonnet behind?

POETESS

At verses she was not inept,
  Her feet were neatly numbered.
She never cried, she softly wept,
  She never slept, she slumbered.

She never ate and rarely dined,
  Her tongue found sweetmeats sour.
She never guessed, but oft divined
  The secrets of a flower.

A flower! Fragrant, pliant, clean,
  More dear to her than crystal.
She knew what yearnings dozed between
  The stamen and the pistil.

Dawn took her thither to the wood,
  At even, home she hithered.
Ah, to the gentle Pan is good—
  She never died, she withered.

POOEM

Writing here last autumn of my hopes of seeing a hoopoe . . .

—*Sir Stephen Tallents in the London* Times

I, too, once hoped to have a hoopoe
Wing its way within my scoopoe,
Crested, quick, and heliotroopoe,
 Proud *Upupa epops.*
For what seemed an eternity,
I sat upon a grassy sloopoe,
Gazing through a telescoopoe,
Weaving snares of finest roopoe,
 Fit for *Upupa epops.*
At last, one day, there came to me,
Inside a crusty enveloopoe,
This note: "Abandon hope, you doopoe;
The hoopoe is a misanthroopoe.
 (Signed) Your far-off friend, *U. e.*"

CAPACITY

CAPACITY 26 PASSENGERS
—*sign in a bus*

Affable, bibulous,
corpulent, dull,
eager-to-find-a-seat,
formidable,
garrulous, humorous,
icy, jejune,
knockabout, laden-
with-luggage (maroon),
mild-mannered, narrow-necked,
oval-eyed, pert,
querulous, rakish,
seductive, tart, vert-
iginous, willowy,
xanthic (or yellow),
young, zebuesque are my
passengers fellow.

24

AN IMAGINABLE CONFERENCE

MR. HENRY GREEN, INDUSTRIALIST, AND MR. WALLACE STEVENS,
VICE-PRESIDENT OF THE HARTFORD ACCIDENT & INDEMNITY CO.,
MEET IN THE COURSE OF BUSINESS

Exchanging gentle grips, the men retire,
prologued by courteous bumbling at the door,
retreat to where a rare room deep exists
on an odd floor, subtly carpeted. The walls

wear charts like checkered vests and blotters ape
the green of cricket fields. Glass multiplies
the pausing men to twice infinity.
An inkstand of blue marble has been carven:

no young girl's wrist is more discreetly veined.
An office boy misplaced and slack intrudes,
apologizes speaking without commas
"Oh sorry sirs I thought" which signifies

what wellmeant wimbly wambly stuff it is
we seem to be made of. Beyond the room,
a gander sun's pure rhetoric ferments
imbroglios of bloom. The stone is so.

The pair confers in murmurings, with words
select and Sunday-soft. No more is known,
but rumor goes that as they hatched the deal,
vistas of lilac weighted their shrewd lids.

THE STORY OF MY LIFE

Fernando Valenti, enthusiast, Yale graduate, and himself represented by numerous recordings of Scarlatti.
—*Saturday Review*

Enthused I went to Yale, enthused
I graduated. Still infused
With this enthusiasm when
Scarlatti called, I answered en-
Thusiastically, and thus
I made recordings numerous,
So numerous that I am classed,
Quite simply, as "enthusiast."

THE NEWLYWEDS

After a one-day honeymoon, the Fishers rushed off to a soft drink bottlers' convention, then on to a ball game, a TV rehearsal and a movie preview.

—Life

"We're married," said Eddie.
Said Debbie, "Incredi-

ble! When is our honey-
moon?" "Over and done," he

replied. "Feeling logy?
Drink Coke." "Look at Yogi

go!" Debbie cried. "Groovy!"
"Rehearsal?" "The movie."

"Some weddie," said Debbie.
Said Eddie, "Yeah, mebbe."

HUMANITIES COURSE

Professor Varder handles Dante
  With wry respect; while one can see
It's all a lie, one must admit
  The "beauty" of the "imagery."

Professor Varder slyly smiles,
  Describing Hegel as a "sage;"
Still, the man has value—he
  Reflects the "temper" of his "age."

Montaigne, Tom Paine, St. Augustine:
  Although their notions came to naught,
They still are "crucial figures" in
  The "pageantry" of "Western thought."

ENGLISH TRAIN COMPARTMENT

These faces make a chapel where worship comes easy:
Homo enim naturaliter est animal sociale.

The flutter of a *Guardian,* the riveted image
of Combe-in-Teignhead, faded by decades of eyes,
the sting of smoke, the coughs, the whispering
lend flavor to piety's honest bone.

Half-sick, we suck our teeth, consult our thumbs,
through brown-stained glass confront the barbered hills
and tailored trees of a tame and castrate land.
Sheep elegant enough for any eclogue
browse under Constable clouds. The unnatural
darkness swells, and passengers stir
at the sound of tapping fingernails. Rain,
beginning, hyphenates our racing windows.

Hands and smiles are freed by the benediction's close.
The lights, always on, now tell. One man talks,
and the water, sluicing sideways, teases our direction.
Indeed, we are lively, smug, and brave
as adventurers safe after some great hazard,
while beside our shoulders the landscape streams
as across the eye of a bathysphere surfacing.

TIME'S FOOL

Frederick Alexander Pott
arrives at parties on the dot.
The drinks have not been mixed, the wife
is still applying, with a knife,
extract of shrimp and chicken spread
to parallelograms of bread
when Pott appears, remarking, "I'm
afraid I'm barging in on time."

Frederick Pott is never late
for any rendezvous or date.
Arrange to meet at some hotel;
you'll find he's been there since the bell
tolled the appointed hour. Not
intending to embarrass, Pott
says shyly, "Punctuality
is psychological with me."

Pott takes the most preposterous pains
to suit the scheduled times of trains.
He goes to concerts, races, plays,
allowing nicely for delays,
and at the age three score and ten
Pott plans to perish; doubtless then
he'll ask, as he has often done,
"This *was* the time agreed upon?"

PHILOLOGICAL

The British puss demurely mews;
His transatlantic kin meow.
The kine in Minnesota moo;
Not so the gentle Devon cows:
      They low,
As every school child ought to know.

TO AN USHERETTE

Ah come with me,
Petite chérie,
And we shall rather happy be.
I know a modest luncheonette
Where, for a little, one can get
A choplet, baby Lima beans,
And, segmented, two tangerines.

Le coup de grâce,
My petty lass,
Will be a demi-demitasse
Within a serviette conveyed
By weazened waiters, underpaid,
Who mincingly might grant us spoons
While a combo tinkles trivial tunes.

Ah with me come,
Ma faible femme,
And I shall say I love you some.

SUNGLASSES

On an olive beach, beneath a turquoise sky
And a limeade sun, by a lurid sea,
While the beryl clouds went blithely by,
We ensconced ourselves, my love and me.

O her verdant hair! and her aqua smile!
O my soul, afloat in an emerald bliss
That retained its tint all the watery while—
And her copper skin, all verdigris!

CLOUD SHADOWS
(New Hampshire)

I

That white coconut, the sun,
  is hidden by his blue leaves,
piratical great galleons.

Our sky their spanking sea,
  they thrust us to an ocean floor,
withal with certain courtesy.

II

These courtly cotton-bellies rub
  around the jewel we live within
and down to the muddled hub

drop complements.
  Down shafts of violet fall
counterweights of shadow, hence

brown, blue, and gray occur
  upon the chipmunk-colored
earth's ruffled fur.

III

Pine islands in a broken lake.
　Beyond Laconia the hills,
islanded by shadows, take

in cooling middle distance
　a motion from above, and lo!
grave mountains belly dance.

A MODEST MOUND OF BONES
(Pennsylvania)

That short-sleeved man, our
   uncle owns
the farm next our farm, south
   and west of us, and
he butchers for a living, hand-to-mouth.
   Once walking on his land
we found a hill, topped by a flower,
   a hill of bones.

They were rain-scrubbed clean,
   lovely things.
Depending how the white
   sun struck, chips of col-
or (green, yellow, dove-blue, a light
   bay) flew off the sul-
len stilled turning there. To have seen
   those clickless rings,

those prisonerless
   ribs, complex
beyond the lathe's loose jaws,
   convolute compounds
of knobs, rods, hooks, moons, absurd paws,
   subtle flats and rounds:
no man could conceive such finesse,
   concave or -vex.

Some warp like umbrella
    handles, keys
to mammoth locks. Some bend
    like equations hunting
infinity, toward which to tend.
    How it sags!—what bunting
is flesh to be hung from such ele-
    gant balconies?

YOUTH'S PROGRESS

Dick Schneider of Wisconsin . . . was elected "Greek
God" for an interfraternity ball.

—Life

When I was born, my mother taped my ears
So they lay flat. When I had aged ten years,
My teeth were firmly braced and much improved.
Two years went by; my tonsils were removed.

At fourteen, I began to comb my hair
A fancy way. Though nothing much was there,
I shaved my upper lip—next year, my chin.
At seventeen, the freckles left my skin.

Just turned nineteen, a nicely molded lad,
I said goodbye to Sis and Mother; Dad
Drove me to Wisconsin and set me loose.
At twenty-one, I was elected Zeus.

DILEMMA IN THE DELTA

An extra quarter-inch on Cleopatra's nose would have
changed the entire course of history.
—*Pascal, misquoted in a newspaper*

Osiris pales; the palace walls
Blush east; through slatted arches falls
The sun, who stripes the cushions where
Empires have been tucked away;
Light fills her jewels and rims her hair
And Cleopatra ripens into day.

Awake, she flings her parakeets
Some chips of cinnamon, and beats
Her scented slave, a lovely thing
Who chokes back almond tears. The queen,
Her wrist fatigued, then bids them bring
Her mirror, a mammoth aquamarine.

She rests the gem upon her thighs
And checks her features. First, the eyes:
Weight them with ink. The lips need rose
Tint: crush a rose. And something's wrong
Between her mouth and brow—her nose,
Her nose seems odd, too long. It *is* too long!

These stupid jokes of Ra! She sees,
Through veils of fury, centuries
Shifting like stirred-up camels. Men

39

Who wrought great deeds remain unborn,
Unthought-of heroes fight like ten,
And her own name is lost to praise or scorn.

While she lies limp, seduced by grief,
There enters, tall beyond belief,
Marc Antony, bronze-braceleted,
Conceived where Rome on Tiber sits.
Six sprigs of laurel gird his head.
His mouth is fat with avocado pits.

"Now dies," she cries, "your love, my fame!
My face shall never seem the same!"
But Marc responds, "*Deorum artis
Laudemus! Bonum hoc est omen.*
Egyptian though your cryptic heart is,
I can't resist a nose so nobly Roman."

A WOODEN DARNING EGG

The carpentered hen
unhinges her wings,
abandons her nest
of splinters, and sings.

    The egg she has laid
    is maple and hard
    as a tenpenny nail
    and smooth as a board.

The grain of the wood
embraces the shape
as brown feathers do
the rooster's round nape.

    Pressured by pride,
    her sandpapered throat
    unwarps when she cries
    Cross-cut! ka-ross-cut!

Beginning to brood
she tests with a level
the angle, sits down,
and coos *Bevel bevel*.

MR. HIGH-MIND

Then went the Jury out, whose names were Mr. *Blind-man*, Mr. *No-good*, Mr. *Malice*, Mr. *Love-lust*, Mr. *Live-loose*, Mr. *Heady*, Mr. *High-mind*, Mr. *Enmity*, Mr. *Lyar*, Mr. *Cruelty*, Mr. *Hate-light*, and Mr. *Implacable*.

—*The Pilgrim's Progress*

Eleven rogues and he to judge a fool—
He files out with the jury, but distaste
Constricts his fluting nostrils, and his cool
Mind turns tepid with contempt. There is brought
A basin for him, in which to wash his hands.
Laving his palms and fingertips, he finds
An image of his white, proportioned thought
Plunged in the squalid suds of other minds.
Unmoved by Lust's requests or Hate's commands
Or Superstition's half-embarrassed bribe,
His brain takes wing and flutters up the course
First plotted by the Greeks, up toward the sphere
Where issues and alternatives are placed
In that remorseless light that knows no source.

Here, in this banana-colored void,
The wise alone have cause for breathing; here
Lines parallel on earth, extended, meet.
Here priests in tweeds gyrate around the feet
Of Fact, their bride, and hymn their gratitude
That each toe of her ten is understood.
From this great height, the notion of the Good

Is seen to be a vulgar one, and crude.
High-mind as Judge descends to Earth, annoyed,
Despairing Justice. Man, a massy tribe,
Cannot possess one wide and neutral eye.
He casts his well-weighted verdict with a sigh
And for a passing moment is distressed
To see it coinciding with the rest.

THE ONE-YEAR-OLD

(After reading the appropriate chapter in *Infant and Child in the Culture of Today,* by Arnold Gesell and Frances Ilg)

Wakes wet; is promptly toileted;
Jargons to himself; is fed;

Executively grips a cup;
Quadrupedal, will sit up

Unaided; laughs; applauds; enjoys
Baths and manipulative toys;

Socializes (parents: shun
Excess acculturation);

Demonstrates prehension; will
Masticate yet seldom spill;

Creeps (gross motor drives are strong);
And jargons, jargons all day long.

SUPERMAN

I drive my car to supermarket,
  The way I take is superhigh,
A superlot is where I park it,
  And Super Suds are what I buy.

Supersalesmen sell me tonic—
  Super-Tone-O, for Relief.
The planes I ride are supersonic.
  In trains, I like the Super Chief.

Supercilious men and women
  Call me superficial—*me*,
Who so superbly learned to swim in
  Supercolossality.

Superphosphate-fed foods feed me;
  Superservice keeps me new.
Who would dare to supersede me,
  Super-super-superwho?

PUBLIUS VERGILIUS MARO, THE MADISON AVENUE HICK

> This was in Italy. The year was the thirty-seventh be-
> fore the birth of Christ. The people were mighty
> hungry, for there was a famine in the land.
> —*the beginning of a Heritage Club advertise-*
> *ment, in* The New Yorker, *for* The Georgics

It takes a heap o' pluggin' t' make a classic sell,
Fer folks are mighty up-to-date, an' jittery as hell;
They got no yen to set aroun' with Vergil in their laps
When they kin read the latest news in twenty-four-point caps.

Ye've got t' hit 'em clean an' hard, with simple predicates,
An' keep the clauses short becuz these days nobody waits
T' foller out a sentence thet all-likely lacks a punch
When in the time o' readin' they could grab a bite o' lunch.

Ye've got t' hand 'em place an' time, an' then a pinch o' slang
T' make 'em feel right comfy in a Latinate shebang,
An' ef your taste buds curdle an' your tum turns queasy—well,
It takes a heap o' pluggin' t' make a classic sell.

IN MEMORIAM

In the novel he marries Victoria but in the movie he
dies.

—caption in Life

Fate lifts us up so she can hurl
   Us down from heights of pride,
Viz.: in the book he got the girl
   But in the movie, died.

The author, seeing he was brave
   And good, rewarded him,
Then, greedy, sold him as a slave
   To savage M-G-M.

He perished on the screen, but thrives
   In print, where serifs keep
Watch o'er the happier of his lives:
   Say, Does he wake, or sleep?

PLANTING A MAILBOX

Prepare the ground when maple buds have burst
  And when the daytime moon is sliced so thin
His fibers drink blue sky with litmus thirst.
  This moment come, begin.

The site should be within an easy walk,
  Beside a road, in stony earth. Your strength
Dictates how deep you delve. The seedling's stalk
  Should show three feet of length.

Don't harrow, weed, or water; just apply
  A little gravel. Sun, and motor fumes
Perform the miracle: in late July,
  A young post office blooms.

TSOKADZE O ALTITUDO

"Tsokadze has invented a new style—apparently without knowing it. He does not bend from the waist at all. His body is straight and relaxed and leaning far out over his skis until his face is only two feet above them, his arms at his side, his head up. His bindings and shoes are so loose that only his toes touch his skies. He gets enormous distances and his flight is so beautiful."

—*Thorlief Schjelderup, quoted in the* Times, *of a young Russian ski-jumper*

Tzokadze leans unknowingly
   Above his skis, relaxed and tall.
   He bends not from the waist at all.
This is the way a man should ski.

He sinks; he rises, up and up,
   His face two feet above the wood.
   This way of jumping, it is good,
Says expert Thorlief Schjelderup.

Beneath his nose, the ski-tips shake;
   He plummets down the deepening wide
   Bright pit of air, arms at his side,
His heart aloft for Russia's sake.

Loose are the bindings, taut the knees,
   Relaxed the man—see, still he flies
   And only his toes touch his skies!
Ah, c'est beau, when Tsokadze skis.

LITTLE POEMS

Overcome, Kim flees in bitter frustration to her TV
studio dressing room where she angrily flings a vase of
flowers to the floor and sobs in abandon to a rose she
destroys: "I'm tearing this flower apart like I'm de-
stroying my life." As she often does, she later turned
the episode into a little poem.

—photograph caption in Life

I woke up tousled, one strap falling
    Off the shoulder, casually.
In came ten *Time-Life* lensmen, calling,
    "Novak, hold that *déshabillé!*"

I went to breakfast, asked for cocoa,
    Prunes, and toast. "Too dark," they said.
"The film we use is Pallid-Foc-O.
    Order peaches, tea, and bread."

I wrote a memo, "To my agent—"
    "Write instead," they said, " 'Dear Mum.' "
In conference, when I made a cogent
    Point, they cried, "No, no! Act dumb."

I told a rose, "I tear you as I
    Tear my life," and heard them say,
"Afraid that 'as' of yours is quasi-
    Classy. We like 'like.' O.K.?"

I dined with friends. The *Time-Life* crewmen
　　Interrupted: "Bare your knees,
Project your bosom, and, for human
　　Interest, look ill at ease."

I, weary, fled to bed. They hounded
　　Me with meters, tripods, eyes
Of Polaroid—I was surrounded!
　　The caption read, "ALONE, Kim cries."

TAO IN THE YANKEE STADIUM BLEACHERS

Distance brings proportion. From here
the populated tiers
as much as players seem part of the show:
a constructed stage beast, three folds of Dante's rose,
or a Chinese military hat
cunningly chased with bodies.
'Falling from his chariot, a drunk man is unhurt
because his soul is intact. Not knowing his fall,
he is unastonished, he is invulnerable.'
So, too, the 'pure man'—'pure'
in the sense of undisturbed water.

'It is not necessary to seek out
a wasteland, swamp, or thicket.'
The old men who saw Hans Wagner
scoop them up in lobster-hands,
the opposing pitcher's pertinent hesitations,
the sky, this meadow, Mantle's thick baked neck,
the old men who in the changing rosters see
a personal mutability,
green slats, wet stone are all to me
as when an emperor commands
a performance with a gesture of his eyes.

'No king on his throne has the joy of the dead,'
the skull told Chuang-tzu.
The thought of death is peppermint to you

when games begin with patriotic song
and a democratic sun beats broadly down.
The Inner Journey seems unjudgeably long
when small boys purchase cups of ice
and, distant as a paradise,
experts, passionate and deft,
wait while Berra flies to left.

DUE RESPECT

They [members of teen-age gangs] are respectful of
their parents and particularly of their mothers—known
as "moo" in their jargon.

—*New York Times Magazine*

Come moo, dear moo, let's you and me
Sit down awhile and talk togee;
My broo's at school, and faa's away
A-gaaing rosebuds while he may.

Of whence we come and whii we go
Most moos nee know nor care to know,
But you are not like any oo:
You're always getting in a poo

Or working up a dreadful laa
Over nothing—nothing. Bah!
Relax. You love me, I love you,
And that's the way it shapes up, moo.

TAX-FREE ENCOUNTER

We have $3,000 savings to invest and believe in the dignity of man. Box Y-920.
—*Personal notice in the* Saturday Review

I met a fellow in whose hand
Was hotly held a cool three grand.
"Inform me of," he said, "the best
Technique of gaining interest."

"Lend money at usurious rates,"
I said. "It soon accumulates."
"Oh no!" he said. "It is unsound
Artistically. Read Ezra Pound."

"Invest," I then suggested. "Deal
Yourself a hand in U.S. Steel."
He snapped, "Big businessmen are sharks.
Peruse *Das Kapital,* by Marx."

"Then buy some U.S. Savings Bonds,
For Our Defense, which corresponds
To Yours and Mine." He told me, "Cease!
Defense degrades. Read *War and Peace.*"

He added, "Dignity of men
Is what we most believe in." Then
He slyly smiled and slowly backed
Away, his principal intact.

ROOM 28

Remembered as octagonal, dark-panelled,
   And never frequented, except by me—
      Indeed, a bower
Attained down avenues where, framed and annalled,
   Great England's great with truculence outlive
      Their hour
And, pigmented, endure mean immortality—
   The room gave rest as some libraries give.

The visitor, approaching, brushed a girlish
   Bust of Lord Byron. Sir James George Frazer's head,
      An unarmed sentry,
Austere, tormented, brazen-browed, and churlish,
   Guarded with sternness fit for Stygian gates
      The entry
To harmless walls where men of letters lately dead
   Were hung. The envied spot was held by Yeats.

His mask, alone a mask among the paintings,
   Attracted to itself what little sun
      The sky admitted.
Half-bronze, half-black, his Janus-face at matins
   Amazed that dim arena of the less
      Weird-witted
Survivors of a blurred time: presbyters upon
   Whose faces grieved the ghost of Earnestness.

56

The whites of Rider Haggard's eyes were showing
    When last I saw them. Conrad's cheeks were green,
        And Rudyard Kipling's
Pink profile burned against his brown works, glowing
    With royalties and realism. Fine
        Sweet stipplings
Limned the long locks that Ellen Terry, seventeen,
    Pre-Raphaelite, and blonde, let down to shine.

There Stevenson looked ill and ill-depicted;
    Frail Patmore, plucked yet gamey; Henry James,
        Our good grammarian,
More paunched and politic than I'd expected.
    Among the lone-faced portraits loomed a trin-
        itarian
Composite: Baring, Chesterton, Belloc. The frame's
    Embellished foursquare dogma boxed them in.

Brave room! Where are they now? In college courses,
    Perused in inferior light, then laid
        On library tables.
Green knights mismounted on empirical horses,
    Encumbered by old armor and a heraldry
        Of labels,
Their universe did not deserve their vows. They fade
    In pale sun, at rest in neither century.

THE SENSUALIST

Each Disc contains not more than ½ minim of Chloroform together with Capsicum, Peppermint, Anise,
Cubeb, Licorice and Linseed.
                    —*from a box of Parke-Davis throat discs*

Come, Capsicum, cast off thy membranous pods;
Thy Guinea girlhood's blossoms have been dried.
Come, Peppermint, belovèd of the gods
(That is, of Hades; Ceres, in her pride,
So Strabo says, transmogrified
Delicious Mintha, making her a plant).

Come, Anise, sweet stomachic stimulant,
Most umbelliferous of condiments,
Depart thy native haunt, the hot Levant.
Swart Licorice, or Liquorice, come hence,
And Linseed, too, of these ingredients
Most colorless, most odorless, most nil.

And Javan Cubeb, come—thy smokable
Gray pericarps and pungent seeds shall be
Our feast's incense. Come, Chloroform, née Phyll,
In demiminims dance unto the spree.
Compounded spices, come: dissolve in me.

SNAPSHOTS

How good of Mrs. Metz! The blur
Must be your cousin Christopher.

A scenic shot Jim took near Lyme.
Those rocks seemed lovely at the time.

And here's a product of the days
When Jim went through his gnarled tree phase.

The man behind the man in shorts—
His name is Shorer, Shaw, or Schwartz.

The kids at play. This must be Keith.
Can that be Wilma underneath?

I'd give my life to know why Josh
Sat next to Mrs. McIntosh.

Jim looked so well in checkered clothes.
I was much slimmer than this shows.

Yes, Jim and I were so in love.
That hat: what *was* I thinking of?

This disappointed Mrs. Striker.
I don't know why, it's very like her.

The dog is Skip. He loved to play.
We had to have him put away.

I guess these people are the Wrens.
There was some water on the lens.

This place is where I was inspired
To—stop me, if your eyes are tired.

MOUNTAIN IMPASSE

"I despise mountains," Stravinsky declared contemptuously, "they don't tell me anything."

—Life

Stravinsky looks upon the mountain,
  The mountain looks on him;
They look (the mountain and Stravinsky)
  And both their views are dim.

"You bore me, mountain," says Stravinsky,
  "I find you dull, and I
Despise you!" Says the mountain:
  "Stravinsky, tell me why."

Stravinsky bellows at the mountain
  And near-by valleys ring:
"You don't confide in me—Stravinsky!
  You never tell me anything!"

The hill is still before Stravinsky.
  The skies in silence glisten.
At last, a rumble, then the mountain:
  "Igor, you never listen."

A BITTER LIFE

Dr. Ycas [of the Quartermaster Research and Development Center, in a report to the National Academy of Sciences] holds that the ocean itself was alive. There were no living creatures in it.

—*New York Times*

O you Dr. Ycas you!
  In one convulsive motion
Your brain has given birth unto
  A viable young ocean.
All monsters pale beside the new:
  The Hydra, Hap, Garuda, Ra,
Italapas, Seb, Hua-hu
  Tiao, Gulltopr, Grendel's ma,
Quetzalcoatl, Kukulkan,
  Onniont, Audhumbla, Ix,
Geryon, Leviathan,
  666,
The ox Ahura Mazda made,
  The Fomors, deevs, Graiae,
And others of this ilk all fade
  Alongside Ycas' sea.
The straits were sinews, channelways
  Were veins, and islands eyes,
Rivers tails, reefs bones, and bays,
  Depending on their size,
Fists, shoulders, heads, ears, mouths, or feet.
  The fjords, as fingers, froze

Sometimes, as did the arctic pate
    And pale antarctic toes.
Horrid, horrid Ocean! The
    Foul grandmother of Tyr,
Who had nine hundred crania,
    Did not look half so queer.
It whistled with a mournful hiss
    In darkness; scared and bored,
It lapped the land, yet every kiss
    Was stonily ignored.
A spheric skin, or blue-green hide,
    Alone the ocean kept
Our planet's house, yet when it died
    One aeon, no one wept.

Hap: Apis, bull-god of Egypt, reincarnation of Osiris. *Garuda:* man-bird, steed of Vishnu, Hindu. *Italapas:* coyote, one of chief Chinook Indian deities. *Seb:* otherwise Geb, Keb, or Qeb; divine goose, Egyptian. *Hua-hu Tiao:* Protean creature, snake or white rat, has the power to assume the shape of a man-eating elephant with wings, etc., Chinese. *Gulltopr:* also Goldropf; Heimdall's horse, Teutonic. *Quetzalcoatl:* name means "serpent dressed with green feathers," though he was, of course, an anthropomorphic god, Aztec. *Kukulkan:* again, feathered serpent, Maya. *Onniont:* monster snake worshiped by Huron Indians. *Audhumbla:* cow who nourished Ymir, the first giant; both sprang from the mist, Norse. *Ix:* one of the four Bacabs, who stood at the four corners of the world and held it up, Maya. *Geryon:* three heads, three bodies, enormous wings, son of Chrysaor and Cillirrhoe, lived on Erythia, Greek. *666:* beast of Revelation 13. *The ox Ahura Mazda made:* a raging, senseless creature; the first creative effort in the animal line made by the Persian Lord of Wisdom. *Fomors:* hideous misshapen monsters representing the kingdom of darkness, Celtic. *deevs:* Persian evil spirits, huge and ugly; long horns, tails, and fangs. *Graiae:* homely women, had only one tooth among them, Greek.

GLASSES

I wear them. They help me. But I
Don't care for them. Two birds, steel hinges
Haunt each an edge of the small sky
My green eyes make. Rim-horn impinges
Upon my vision's furry fringes;
Faint dust collects upon the dry,
Unblinking shield behind which cringes
My naked, deprecated eye.

My gaze feels aimed. It is as if
Two manufactured beams had been
Lodged in my sockets—hollow, stiff,
And gray, like mailing tubes—and when
I pivot, vases topple down
From tabletops, and women frown.

A RACK OF PAPERBACKS

Gateway, Grove,
  and Dover say,
"Unamuno
  any day."

Beacon Press
  and Torchlight chorus,
"Kierkegaard
  does nicely for us."

"Willey, Waley,"
  Anchor bleats,
"Auden, Barzun,
  Kazin, Keats."

"Tovey, Glover,
  Cohen, Fry"
is Meridi-
  an's reply.

"Bentley's best,"
  brags Dramabooks.
Harvest burgeons
  Cleanth Brooks.

All, including
   Sentinel,
Jaico, Maco,
   Arco, Dell,

Noonday, Vintage,
   Living Age,
Mentor, Wisdom—
   page on page

of classics much
   too little known
when books were big
   and bindings sewn—

agree: "Lord Raglan,
   Margaret Mead,
Moses Hadas,
   Herbert Read,

the Panchatantra,
   Hamsun's 'Pan,'
Tillich, Ilg,
   Kahlil Gibran,

and Henry James
   sell better if
their spines are not
   austerely stiff."

POPULAR REVIVALS, 1956

The thylacine, long thought to be extinct,
Is not. The ancient dog-like creature, linked
To kangaroos and platypi, still pounces
On his Tasmanian prey, the *Times* announces.

The tarpan (stumpy, prehistoric horse)
Has been rebred—in Germany, of course.
Herr Heinz Heck, by striking genetic chords,
Has out of plowmares beat his tiny wards.

The California fur seal, a refined
And gullible amphibian consigned
By profit-seeking sealers to perdition,
Barked at the recent Gilmore expedition.

The bison, butchered on our Western prairie,
Took refuge in our coinage. Now, contrary
To what was feared, the herds are out of danger
And in the films, co-starred with Stewart Granger.

ODE III.ii : HORACE

Let the boy, timber-tough from vigorous soldiering,
learn to endure lack amicably,
and let him, horseman feared for his javelin,
plague the ferocious men of Parthos;

let him live his life lower than heaven
in the midst of restless things. Seeing him
from enemy ramparts, may the warring tyrant's wife
and the young ripe woman breathe, "Ah,

let not our kingly lover, clumsy
in the swirl of combat, stroke the lion
rough to the touch, whom fury for blood
thrusts through the thick of the slaughter!"

Sweet it is, and seemly, to die for country.
Death overtakes the runaway as well,
and does not spare the coward backs
and knees of youths who are not warlike.

Manliness, not knowing the taint of defeat,
flashes forth with unsullied glory,
neither lifts nor lowers the axes
at a whisper from the scatterbrained mob.

Manliness, that throws open heaven to those
undeserving of death, plots its course

by a route denied to most, and on pinion
soaring scorns the common crowd, the damp earth.

There is, for faithful silence, too,
sure reward. I will forbid the man who spreads abroad
occult Ceres' sacred rites
to exist beneath a roof or to unmoor a frail craft

with me. Often slighted Jupiter
involves the unpolluted with the impure;
rarely does Poena not catch the wicked man,
though he has the head start, and her step is hesitant.

A CHEERFUL ALPHABET OF PLEASANT OBJECTS

to David, for his edification

Aᴘᴘʟᴇ

Since Time began, such alphabets begin
With Apple, source of Knowledge and of Sin.
My child, take heart: the fruit that undid Man
Brought out as well the best in Paul Cézanne.

Bɪʀᴅʙᴀᴛʜ

The birdbath is a placid eye
Beneath the apple trees; the sky
Is by the birdbath seldom seen,
And hence its water is brown-green.

When blackbirds come to purge their wings,
The water darkens; one wren brings
A touch of rust; the oriole
Casts down a casual aureole.

Trees ripen; then the birdbath glows
With muddled hints of gold and rose.
Leaves fall, and thus unveil the sky;
But now the birdbath is bone dry.

70

Cog

Not for him the darkly planned
   Ambiguities of flesh.
His maker gave him one command:
   Mesh.

Doily

Along the upland meadows
   of the dining-table bloom
the doilies, openfaced and
   white; within the living-room
they cling to every slope of
   chair, and every chic plateau.
Around the trunks of lamps whose
   shades exude a healthy glow,
the doily spreads her petals
   made of ivory and cream.
Hands off! Who plucks a doily
   rattles Nature's farflung Scheme.

Easy chair

Avoid the clicking three-way lamp; beware
   The throw rug's coils, the two-faced sofabed,
   The vile lowboy; but more than any, dread
The hippopotomastic easy chair.

For, seated, you shall sink and never rise.
   The slow osmosis of the chair's embrace
   Shall make your arms *its* arms, and make your face
An antimacassar monogrammed with eyes.

71

Flowerpot

This clayey fez,
inverted, is
a shoe for roots:
an orange boot

wherein one leg
goes down to beg
more dirt. Alas,
in vain it asks.

Geranium

Who has this home?
Geranium,
a maiden plant
and aspirant

to broader green.
Against the screen
she leans her head,
inhibited.

More Dirt (the moral runs) or Else We Wane—
See D. H. Lawrence, Ovid, or Mark Twain.

Hairbrush

Made of hair,
it brushes locks
of hair:
      and there,
my son,
you have a Chinese paradox,
but not much of one.

Icebox

In Daddy's day there were such things:
   Wood cabinets of cool
In which a cake of ice was placed
   While he was off at school.

Blue-veined, partitioned in itself,
   The cake seemed cut of air
Which had exploded; one cracked star
   Appeared imprisoned there.

The corners wore throughout the day;
   The slats whereon it rested
Seeped upwards, so the slippery base
   Became severely crested.

Eventually an egg so small
   It could be tossed away,
The ice cake vanished quite, as has
   That rather distant day.

Jack

A card, a toy, a hoist,
a flag, a stay, a fruit,
a sailor, John, a pot,
a rabbit, knife, and boot;
o'-lantern, in-the-box
or -pulpit, Ketch, a daw,
a-dandy, of-all-trades,
anapes, an ass, a straw.

73

KNOB

Conceptually a blob,
the knob
is a smallish object which,
hitched
to a larger,
acts as verger.

It enables
us to gain access to drawers in end tables;
it shepherds
us into cupboards.

Prouder than buttons yet humbler than handles
knobs avoid scandals
and keep themselves stiff.
When one (as on a bedpost) turns decorative, it is as if
Everyman were to
become a chorine in a Broadway revue.

LETTER SLOT

Once a day this broad mouth spews
Apologies, bills, rags, and news.

Mirror

When you look	kool uoy nehW
into a mirror	rorrim a otni
it is not	ton si ti
yourself you see,	,ees uoy flesruoy
but a kind	dnik a tub
of apish error	rorre hsipa fo
posed in fearful	lufraef ni desop
symmetry.	yrtemmys

Nutcracker

His teeth are part of his shoulders because
A   nut
Is broken best by arms that serve as jaws.

Oᴛᴛᴏᴍᴀɴ

Lessons in history: the Greeks
Were once more civilized than Swedes.
Iranians were, for several weeks,
    Invincible, as Medes.

The mild Mongolians, on a spree,
Beheaded half of Asia; and
The Arabs, in their century,
    Subdued a world of sand.

Just so, the cushioned stool we deign
To sit on, called the Ottoman:
We would not dare, were this the reign
    Of Sultan Selim Khan.

From India to Hungary
The Ottoman held sway; his scope
Extended well into the sea
    And terrified the Pope.

And Bulgar, Mameluke, and Moor
All hastened to kowtow
To tasseled bits of furniture.
    It seems fantastic now.

Pendulum

This lean commuter busies

Himself with being steady;

No matter where he is, he's

Been there much already.

Q<small>UILT</small>

The quilt that covers all of us, to date,
Has patches numbered 1 to 48,
Five northern rents, a crooked central seam,
    A ragged eastern edge, a way
    Of bunching uglily, and a
Perhaps too energetic color scheme.

Though shaken every twenty years, this fine
Old quilt was never beaten on the line.
It took long making. Generations passed
    While thread was sought, and calico
    And silk were coaxed from Mexico
And France. The biggest squares were added last.

Don't kick your covers, son. The bed is built
So you can never shake the clinging quilt
That blanketed your birth and tries to keep
    Your waking warm, impalpable
    As atmosphere. As earth it shall
Be tucked about you through your longest sleep.

Rainspout

Up the house's nether corner,
Snaky-skilled, the burglar shinnies,
Peeking, cautious, in the dormer,
Creeping, wary, where the tin is.

Stealthily he starts to burgle.
Hear his underhanded mutter;
Hear him, with a guilty gurgle,
Pour his loot into the gutter.

Stopper

Take instead the honest stopper,
Crying "halt" to running water,
Chained to duty, as is proper
For a piece of rubber mortar.

Dense resistance is the raison
D'être of this dull sentry; certes
He shall hold the brimming basin
Even after water dirties.

Trivet

"What is it? Why?" Thus the trivet,
  Like a piece of algebra,
Embraces mysteries which give it
  Quelque chose, je ne sais quoi.

Umbrella

Pterodactylic complement
  Of black and evil weather,
It lifts on ribbing badly bent
  One wing of threadbare leather.

Don't treat it as a cane. Don't poke
  The end at friends; you're liable
To give offense. Don't stick a spoke
  In anybody's eyeball.

Don't open it within the house
  Or let it lie in barrooms,
Since either oversight will rouse
  Excursions and alarums.

Unfurl it when the heavens burst,
  And hold it over ladies.
Observe taboos; the bird, accurst,
  Was born and reared in Hades.

Vacuum cleaner

This humming broom, with more aplomb
  Than tracts by A. Camus,
Refutes the ancient axiom
  That Nothing has no use.

W<small>HEEL</small>

For all of his undoubted skill
The Inca lacked the wheel until
Pizarro came to high Peru
And said that llamas wouldn't do.

The Eskimos had never heard
Of centripetal force when Byrd
Bicycled up onto a floe
And told them, "This how white man go."

Nepal's Joe Averageperson feels
He should get by on prayer wheels.
The Navajos retread their squaws.
So lucky, lucky you, because

Whereas, below the pyramids
In Africa, some hominids
Have waited since the Pliocene,
You'll get the wheel at age sixteen.

X<small>YSTER</small>

"An instrument for scraping bones"
    Describes the knife.
The word is rarely used—but why?
    What else is life?

Y<small>ARDSTICK</small>

Like Milton's	measuring the	twofold world
in constantly	decasyllabic	pentameters,
the yardstick	trims the epic	of land and air
and has it trip	obsequiously	to trimeters,
each foot made	of just twelve	symbols each.

Z<small>EPPELIN</small>

A German specialty, since men
   Of other nations must inveigle
Helium or hydrogen;
   But Germany had Hegel.

It fell, as do Philosophy's
   Symmetric, portly darlings,
Fell from skies where one still sees
   Religion's narrow starlings.